Times Pub

The Lehigh Valley Comet

Volume 4, no. 1

Times Pub

The Lehigh Valley Comet
Volume 4, no. 1

ISBN/EAN: 9783337202309

Printed in Europe, USA, Canada, Australia, Japan

Cover: Foto ©Andreas Hilbeck / pixelio.de

More available books at **www.hansebooks.com**

THE LEHIGH VALLEY Comet

Vol. IV.   No. 1.

SUMMER, 1891.

AN ILLUSTRATED
QUARTERLY
DEVOTED TO THE INTERESTS of the
LEHIGH,
SCHUYLKILL,
WYOMING,
AND
SUSQUEHANNA
VALLEYS

Historical
Industrial and
Scenic.

H.E BROWN
91.

THIS SPACE TO LET.

THE LEHICH VALLEY COMET.

AN ILLUSTRATED QUARTERLY DEVOTED TO THE DIVERSIFIED INTERESTS OF THE LEHIGH, WYOMING AND SUSQUEHANNA VALLEYS.

H. E. BROWN, ASSOCIATE EDITOR AND ARTIST.	EDITED AND PUBLISHED BY THE PASSENGER DEPARTMENT OF THE LEHIGH VALLEY RAILROAD CO.

SUMMER.	PRESS OF TIMES PUBLISHING CO., BETHLEHEM, PA.	1891.

THE INDIANS OF THE DELAWARE, LEHIGH, SCHUYLKILL, WYOMING AND SUSQUEHANNA, IN THE EARLY, OR COLONIAL, DAYS.

INDIAN GOVERNMENT.

The American Indian a century ago was not the Indian of today. The persecution of the whites has taught that race of noblemen that there was another motive in living besides doing good to your fellow-man. The rum lavishingly dealt out to them by the traders, which enabled them to consummate a better bargain; the treachery of the avaricious among the Dutch when they bought as much land as they could "cover with a bullock's hide," on which to raise greens for their soup, and cutting that hide into a thin thong and *encircling* with it several acres, again taught the Indians a lesson that they have not yet forgotten. The notorious "Indian walk" practiced by the more subtle English was another lesson in political economy that has remained with them, and these subtleties have not enriched us as a nation, but on the contrary, by being permitted, have fostered this sort of iniquity until it is seriously threatening the nation's prosperity and possibly its life. Law is no longer synonymous with equity, and yet none will dare deny that it should be. It is therefore refreshing to turn backward the pages of history and learn, if we may, from the primitive American, how America was ruled before despoiled by tricksters, and, if we can, recover some of the virtues lost to us and it through avaricious knavery. The Indians had no code of laws. Their chiefs were men who studied the welfare of their nation and associated men of experience with them, of whom they cheerfully took counsel. On them the people relied, believing that what they did was for the public good, and it may be stated that their confidence was rarely, if ever, misplaced. When the men in council had fully deliberated and decided finally what course to pursue they assembled the tribe or nation and imparted their purposes. They were at once endorsed and the necessary *wampum* cheerfully given to carry the project in view to a successful end. The chiefs were careful to preserve for their own information and that of future generations all important deliberations and treaties, and could at any time relate, very minutely, what had passed between Wm. Penn and their forefathers at their first meeting and afterwards, as well as any and all deliberations and treaties made with the governors who succeeded him. For the purpose of retaining these the nation assembled twice a year, where the treaties were rehearsed. [This attribute they still retain to a remarkable degree.] On these occasions they always met at a chosen spot in the woods at a short distance from the town, where a fire was kindled and at the proper time provisions were brought out to them. There, on a large piece of bark or a blanket, the documents were laid in such a manner that the reader could as readily determine the sub-divisions as an orator of our day can by the headings. If any paper or parchment writings were connected with the belts or strings of *wampum*, they applied to some trusty white man, such as their spiritual advisers, to read and translate the contents to them. Their speaker, who was always chosen because of his superior talents and especial training, then arose and, in an audible voice, delivered, with the gravity the subject required, sentence after sentence of the contents. By the *turning* of the belts, which occurred after half of the speech had been delivered, the auditors were as fully apprised of the progress being made in the delivery as we could by glancing at the remaining pages of a MS. or the leaves of a book. The belts and strings, when done with

4

THE LEHIGH VALLEY COMET.

KENNARD'S HOTEL,

MESHOPPEN, PA.

Geo. L. Kennard, Prop'r.

Offers the traveling public superior accommodations. Hot and cold water and steam throughout.

Cuisine principally from hotel farm and gardens.

Special accommodation for fishermen. Boats and Guides at all times.

Vol.IV.-4.

ESTABLISHED 1866.

W. R. LAWFER & CO.,

611 and 613 HAMILTON STREET,
608, 610, 612 and 614 Court Street,
14 and 16 N. Sixth Street,

ALLENTOWN, PA.

THE LARGEST AND MOST THOROUGHLY STOCKED STORE IN EASTERN PENNSYLVANIA.

Covering 31,543 Square Feet of Floor Space.

— JOBBERS OF AND RETAIL DEALERS IN —

DRY GOODS, NOTIONS, CARPETS, RUGS, CURTAINS,

Draperies, Shades, Oil Cloth, Linoleum, &c., &c.

SPECIAL ATTENTION GIVEN TO **AWNINGS** FOR PUBLIC BUILDINGS and PRIVATE DWELLINGS.

FURNISHING AND EQUIPMENT OF HOTELS, CLUBS, HOSPITALS, RAILROAD DEPOTS, SCHOOL BUILDINGS, CHURCHES and SOCIETY HALLS SOLICITED.

Reference—THE LEHIGH VALLEY RAILROAD CO.
KEYSTONE NORMAL SCHOOL, Kutztown, Pa.,
MANSION HOUSE, Mauch Chunk, Pa.

Vol. IV-2.

If you have anything useful and WORTH BUYING

ADVERTISE IT IN "THE LEHIGH VALLEY COMET."

THIS SPACE TO LET.

by the speaker, were again handed to the chief, who put them back into the "speech-bag."

A message of importance was generally sent to point of destination by an inferior chief, counsellor or speaker, especially when an immediate answer was expected. In other cases, where, for instance, only an answer to a speech was to be sent, two capable young men were selected, the

communication were, to them, quite as intelligible as our methods are to us. The belts of *wampum* were their documents. These belts were of different dimensions, both in length and] breadth. They were of two colors, viz., white and black, the former denoting that which was good, as peace, friendship, etc., the latter quite the opposite. The pipe, being of red clay, had to be whitened with

From Plateau PAXINOSA at EASTON PA.

one delivering the answer while the other acted the part of monitor. If the message was of a private nature, they were instructed "to draw it under ground," which meant not to divulge it *en route.* If they were told to enter *into the earth* with the message or speech, and rise again] at the place where it was to have been delivered, the instruction simply meant that they should choose unfrequented ways, avoiding beaten paths, which were, to them, the highway. Chiefs of tribes or nations paid no attention to any *reports.* Not until their attention was called officially to an inter-national or inter-tribal measure did they consider or talk about it. The methods of inter-

white clay before it could be considered a "pipe of peace."

Roads from one friendly nation to another were generally marked on the belts by one or two rows of white *wampum* interwoven with the black running through the middle from 'end to end, and meant that the nations were on friendly terms with each other. A black belt with a hatchet painted on it in red was a war belt. This belt, accompanied with a twist or roll of tobacco, was an invitation to join in a war against a common foe. If the nation to whom such belt and tobacco were sent made answer that it "smoked well" consent was given. If, however, it was declined and no

smoke had, no persuasion would suffice to change their decision. If an attempt was made to coerce a chief by laying the belt and tobacco on his shoulders, he shook it off and with a stick threw it from him as he would a dead snake, never allowing his hand to touch it.

Although their councils did not seat themselves after the manner of civilized people, they were not

THE INDIANS AS SOCIALISTS.

The Mannitto (God) was all in all to the Indian of the past. Not satisfied with paying their first duties to the Lord of all, in the best manner they were able, the Indians also endeavored to fulfil the views they supposed He had in creating the world. They thought that He made the earth and all that it contained for the common good of mankind; when He stocked the country with game He gave sufficient for all, and that it was not intended that a favored few alone should enjoy these gifts. Everything was given in common

wanting in dignity or respect. Faithful to the trust committed to them, they were careless of ceremonies. They sat around the council fire regardless of attitude, but were never wanting in attention. The earnestness attending council deliberations is attested in many instances to have been of a tragic nature; nothing except the attack of an enemy could divert business or attention. When a member of a tribe committed a crime he was at once ostracized and all national interest in his welfare ceased.

to the sons of men. "Whatever liveth on the land, whatsoever groweth out of the earth, all that is in the rivers and waters flowing through the same, was given jointly to all, and every one is entitled to his share."

From this principle hospitality flowed as from its source. With them it was not a virtue, but a strict duty; hence they were never in search of excuses to avoid giving, but freely supplied their neighbors' wants from the stock prepared for their own use. They gave and were hospitable to all,

without exception, and were often known to divide their last morsel with their less favored neighbor or stranger within their gates. Their reasoning was quite orthodox and Christlike. To their minds the meat of the woods and air was common to all: the successful hunter was favored by the Most High. The corn or vegetable grew from the ground, yet not by the power of man, but that of the Great Spirit. Again, on the principle that all descended from one parent, all were of the same family, who, therefore, ought at all times and on all occasions to

AT LAURY'S.

be serviceable and kind to each other, and by that means make themselves acceptable to the Great Mannitto, the head of the universal family. Bishop John Heckewelder gives an illustration of this in his "Indian Narratives:" "Some traveling Indians having, in the year 1777, put their horses over night in my little meadow at Gnaden-hütten on the Muskingum, I called on them in the morning to learn why they had done so. I endeavored to make them sensible of the injury they had done me, especially as I intended to mow the meadow in a day or two. Having finished my complaint, one of them replied: 'My friend, it seems you lay claim to the grass my horses have eaten because you had it enclosed with a fence; now tell me, who caused the grass to grow? Can you make the grass grow? I think not, and nobody can, except the Great Mannitto. He it is who causes it to grow both for your horses and for mine. See, friend, the grass which grows out of the earth is common to all, the game in the woods is common to all. Say, did you never eat venison and bear's meat?' 'Yes, very often.' 'Well, and did you ever hear me or any other Indian complain about that?' 'No.' 'Then be not disturbed at my

horses having eaten, only once, of what you call your grass, though the grass my horses did eat, in like manner as the meat you did eat, was given to the Indians by the Great Spirit. For friendship's sake, however, I shall never put my horses in your meadow again.'"

From the bishop we learn that the Indians were not only just, but that they were also a generous people and could not see the sick and aged suffer for want of anything attainable. Those in want of clothing were at once supplied without any thought of remuneration or reciprocity. When, however, the giving was understood to be in form of a donation, a return, in some measure, was always anticipated. In making presents to strangers some slight token in return, to be a token of remembrance, was all that was looked for. If, however, they gave anything to a trader, they expected at least double the value in return, saying he could afford it, since he had cheated them so often.

EDUCATION.

It has been a subject of wonder how a nation without a written code of laws or system of jurisprudence, without a constitution, without even a single elective or hereditary magistrate, could subsist together in peace and harmony and in the exercise of the moral virtues. Yet these people were well and effectually governed by the mere force of the ascendancy which men of superior minds have over those of ordinary mold. Bishop Heckewelder, an exemplary servant of the Master, was peculiarly endowed with a keen sense of the eternal fitness of things and a more than ordinarily close observer. He has left us the fruits of his observation from a standpoint which is indisputable. From them we learn that he had reason to be satisfied that the cause for the phenomenon could in a great degree be ascribed to the pains which the Indians took to instil, at an early age, honest and virtuous principles into the minds of their children, and to the method they pursued in educating them. They had no system, these sons of nature, who, by following alone her simple dictates, at once discovered without effort that plain, obvious path which the philosophers of the world have been so long in search of.

The first step that parents took toward educating their young was to prepare them for future happiness by impressing upon their tender minds that

H.B BROWN

Glen Onoko

they were indebted for their existence to a great, good and beneficent Spirit, who not only gave them life, but had ordained them for certain great purposes: that He had given them a fertile and extensive country well stocked with game of every kind for their subsistence; and that by one of His inferior spirits He had also sent down to them from above corn, pumpkins, squashes, beans and other vegetables for their nourishment, all of which blessings their ancestors had enjoyed for a great number of ages; that this Great Spirit looked down upon the Indians to see whether they were grateful to Him and made Him a due return for the many benefits He had bestowed; that, therefore, it was their duty to worship Him and do acts pleasing to Him.

After this lesson came others, directing a close observance of the habits and bearing of the representative men of the nation, to which they were to conform themselves. They were also taught to accept the advice of their seniors in good faith, and to be wise and good they must comply with the instructions given by the valiant and experienced of their nation, to look forward to being themselves called wise men, a title to which no Indian was indifferent. The next step in the education of the Indian youth was to impress upon their minds the fact that there was also an evil spirit, who was to be shunned; making them sensible of the difference between good deeds and pernicious habits. This instruction was never given in an authoritative tone, but, on the contrary, in a persuasive manner. The child's pride was the feeling to which an appeal was made. The young were taught to venerate and revere the aged and decrepit by having their attention especially called to kind acts rendered by others, and when a child did a noble act he or she was at once complimented. The whole plan of education had a tendency to elevate rather than to depress the mind, which had the effect of making determined hunters and fearless warriors. When a lad had killed his first deer or bear the parents of others held him up as an example, saying that boy has listened attentively to aged and experienced hunters and has profited by their advice. If, however, a youth was precocious and wilful, he was not shielded, but at once pointed out as one who had ignored all good advice and was determined to bring disgrace and shame upon his peo-

ple, which was equivalent to an admonition to shun such an one's company. Thus did the youth grow to manhood and in turn become clothed with the responsibilities transmitted to him by the aged and infirm. Each and every one grown to man's estate became a teacher by precept and example, in which honor and hospitality were the fundamental stones.

FOOD AND COOKERY.

Those who imagine that the Indian was always a pensioner are sadly misinformed. It is little more than a century ago that their tepees dotted the fertile plains of the Hudson, Delaware, Lehigh, Schuylkill, Wyoming and Susquehanna Valleys. Then game was abundant in the forests, the glades of which were traversed daily by the husband and father in his efforts to supply the demands of those dependent upon his success as a hunter, while the rivers gave forth abundantly most delicious fish. In those early days few encroachments were made upon the "original people," and when the messengers of peace from the mission colony, called Bethlehem, came among these sons of nature, each vied with the other in extending hospitalities. The same good bishop to whom we have been so often indebted has this to say relative to their cooking, and feeling it must be more acceptable in his own language we give it thus: "The principal food of the Indians consists

of the game which they take or kill in the woods, the fish out of the waters, and the maize, potatoes, beans, squashes, cucumbers, melons, and, occasionally, cabbages and turnips, which they raise in their fields. They make use also of various roots of plants, fruits, nuts and berries out of the woods, by way of relish or as a seasoning to their vic-

H.E.BROWN.
91.

tuals, sometimes also from necessity. They commonly make two meals every day, which, they say, are enough. If any one should feel hungry between meal-times, there is generally something in the house ready for him. The hunter prefers going out with his gun on an empty stomach; he says that hunger stimulates him to exertion by reminding him continually of his wants, whereas a full stomach makes a hunter easy, careless and lazy, ever thinking of his home and losing his time to no purpose. With all their industry, nevertheless, and notwithstanding this strong stimulant, many a day passes over their heads that they have not met with any kind of game, nor consequently tasted a morsel of victuals. Still they go on with their chase in hopes of being able to carry some provisions home, and do not give up the pursuit until it is so dark that they can see no longer. The morning and the evening, they say, are the precious hours for the hunter. They lose nothing by sleeping in the middle of the day, that is to say between 10 o'clock in the morning and 4 in the afternoon, except in dark, cloudy weather, when the whole day is nearly equally good for hunting. Therefore, the hunter who happens to have no meat in his house will be off and in the woods before daylight, and strive to be in again before breakfast with a deer, turkey, goose, bear or raccoon, or some other game then in season. Meanwhile, his wife has pounded her corn, now boiling on the fire, and baked her bread, which gives them a good breakfast. If, however, the husband is not returned by 10 o'clock in the forenoon, the family take their meal by themselves and his share is put aside for him until he comes home.

"The Indians have a number of manners of preparing their corn. They make an excellent pottage of it by boiling it with fresh or dried meats (the latter pounded), dried pumpkins, fried beans and chestnuts. They sometimes sweeten it with sugar or molasses from the sugar-maple tree. Another very good dish is prepared by boiling with their corn or maize the washed kernels of the shellbark or hickory-nut. They pound the nuts in a block or mortar, pouring a little water on them and gradually a little more as they become dry, until at last there is a sufficient quantity of water, so that by stirring up the pounded nuts the broken shells separate from the liquor, which,

from the pounded kernels, assumes the appearance of milk. This being put into a kettle and mixed with the pottage, gives it a rich and agreeable flavor. If the broken shells do not all freely separate by swimming on the top or sinking to the bottom, the liquor is strained through a clean cloth before it is put into the kettle. They also prepare a variety of dishes from pumpkins, squash, and the green French or kidney bean; they are very particular in their choice of pumpkins and squashes and in the manner of cooking them. The women say that the less water is put to them the better dish they make, and that it would be still better if they were stewed without any water, merely in the steam of the sap which they contain. They cover up the pots in which they cook them with large leaves of the pumpkin vine, cabbages and other leaves of the larger kinds. They make an excellent preserve from the cranberry and crabapple, to which, after it has been well stewed, they add a proper quantity of sugar or molasses.

"Their bread is of two kinds; one made up of green corn while in the milk, and another of the same grain when fully ripe and quite dry. This last is pounded as fine as possible, then sifted and kneaded into dough, which is afterward made up into cakes of six inches in diameter and about an inch in thickness, rounded off on the edge. In baking these cakes they are extremely particular; the ashes must be clean and hot and, if possible, come out of good, dry oak bark, which, they say, gives a brisk and durable heat. In the dough of this kind of bread they frequently mix boiled pumpkins, green or dried, dry beans or well-pared chestnuts boiled in the same manner, dried venison well pounded, whortle-berries, green or dry, but not boiled, sugar and other palatable ingredients. For the other kind of bread, the green corn, either pounded or mashed, is put in broad green corn blades, generally filled in with a ladle, well wrapped up and baked in the ashes like the other. They consider this a very delicate morsel, but, for me, it is too sweet.

"Their meats they either boil, roast or broil. Their roasting is done by running a wooden spit sharpened at each end through the meat, which they place near the fire and occasionally turn. They broil on clean coals drawn off from the fire for that purpose. They often laugh at white hun-

ters for baking their bread in dirty ashes and being alike careless of cleanliness when they broil their meat. They are fond of dried venison pounded in a mortar and dipped in bear's oil. The Delawares, Mohicans and Shawnees are very particular in their choice of meats, and nothing short of the most pressing hunger can induce them to eat of certain animals, such as the horse, dog, wild-cat, panther, fox, muskrat, wolf, etc., all of which I have seen the Chippewas feast upon with a seemingly good appetite.

"The woods and waters at certain times and seasons furnish an abundant supply of wholesome, nourishing food, which, if carefully gathered, cured and stored up, would serve them for a whole year, but they are not always so provident."

DRESS AND ORNAMEN-
TATION.

In ancient times the dress of the Indians was made of the skins of animals and feathers. This clothing, they said, was not only warmer, but lasted longer than any woolen goods bartered from the white traders. They dressed any skin, even that of the buffalo, so that it became quite soft and supple. A good buffalo or bear skin blanket served them many years with apparently little wear. The beaver and raccoon skin blankets were very pliant, warm and durable; they sewed together as many of these skins as were necessary, carefully setting the hair or fur all the same way, so that the blanket or covering was smooth and readily shed the rain. In the colder or dry weather the blanket was worn with the fur or hair next to the body. During the cold and inclement seasons the women made themselves petticoats of this material, their waists or upper garment being made of dressed deerskin. For the warmer and dry season dressed deerskin was the material out of which the upper and nether garments were made for the females. Thus shirt, skirt, leggings and shoes were provided by the hide of the deer. Each and every one was his or her own currier. The hair was shaved off the skins with knives made out of the large rib bones of the elk and buffalo. The finer sense of the women led them to make blankets composed of feathers, and some of these were truly marvels of

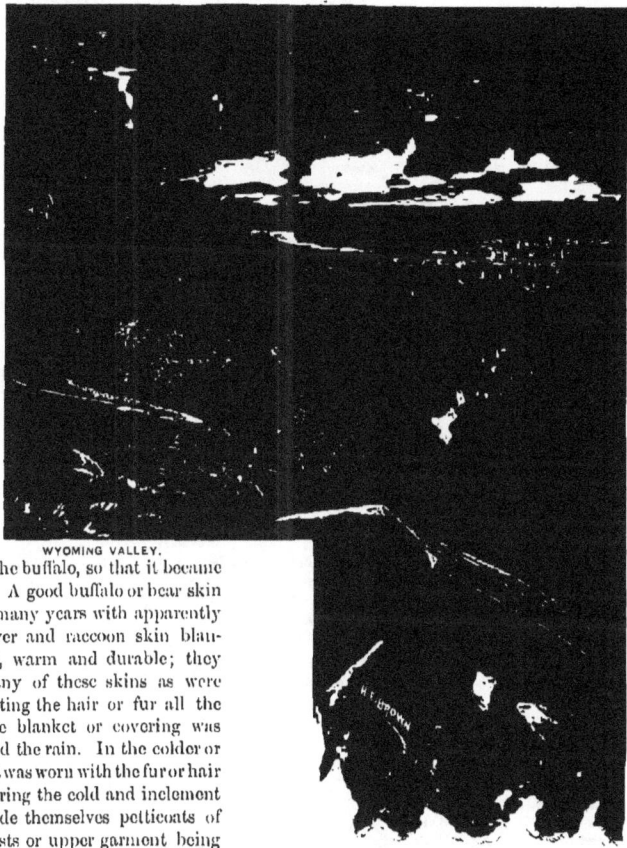

WYOMING VALLEY.

When traveling through the historic Valley of Wyoming, fail not to call for that
CELEBRATED BEVERAGE,

"STEGMAIER'S LIEBOTSCHANER."

Brewery and Office, 230-246 East Market St., WILKES BARRE, PA. Vol.III-4.

SUMMER RESORTS, HOTELS AND BOARDING HOUSES.

Location and Name of Hotel	Proprietor	Rate per Day	Rate per Week	Capacity
New Market, N.J.	Private Families		$5.00 to $7.00	
Clinton, N.J.				
Union House	J. B. Weller	$1.50	7.00	
Clinton House	E. Tomson	1.50	7.00	30
Private Families	—	—	5.00 to 7.00	25
Flemington, N.J.				
County House	W. H. Force, Jr.	2.00	5.00 to 8.00	
Union House	L. Humphrey	2.00	5.00 to 8.00	
Easton, Pa.				
Paxinosa Inn	Chas. A. Stone	4.00	17.50 to 21.00	400
United States Ho.	Geo. H. Vincent	2.50 to 3.00	12.00 to 15.00	100
Franklin House	B. Case	2.00		100
Bethlehem, Pa.				
Wyandotte Hotel	Geo. C. Boldt	2.50	8.00 to 15.00	125
The Eagle Hotel	Mrs. M. B. Hoppes	2.50 to 3.00	10.00	100
The Sun Inn	A. H. Beers	2.00	10., 12 & 15.	150
American House	Geo. S. Christ	1.50	7.00 to 10.00	75
Central House	J. Hagenbuch	1.00	1.50 to 6.00	50
Washington House	Dean Geissinger	1.50	7.00	70
Pacific House	T. F. Marsteller	2.00	9.00	50
Fetter's Hotel	M. C. Fetter	2.00	10.00 to 12.00	50
Allentown, Pa.				
Hotel Allen	J. H. Harris	2.50 to 3.00	12.00 to 15.00	300
American Hotel	H. A. Hayden	2.00 to 2.50	8.00 to 12.00	150
Eagle Hotel	V. D. Barner	1.50	5.00 to 7.00	125
Merchants' Hotel	Edwin Yeager	1.50	5.00 to 7.00	110
Catasauqua, Pa.				
Mansion House	A. S. Fry	2.00	7.00	25
Eagle Hotel	D. Hart	2.00	9.00	30
Laury's.				
Laury's Hotel	Geo. Kimball	1.50	7.00	30
Slatington.				
Bittner House	A. Bittner	2.00	7.00 to 10.00	50
Mauch Chunk.				
Mansion House	J. S. Keiser & Son	2.50 to 3.00	12.00 to 17.00	400
American House	Lafayette Lentz	2.50 to 3.00	10.00 to 15.00	200
Glen Onoko.				
Hotel Wahnetah	W. Seitz	2.50 to 3.00	10.00 to 15.00	200
Hazleton.				
Central Hotel	Wm. Doolittle	2.50	12.00	175
Hazleton Hotel	Mrs. A. E. Coller	2.00	5.00	28
Farmers' Hotel	Geo. Schaeffer	1.00	5.00	35
White Haven.				
White Haven Ho.	Mrs. E. Smith	2.00	10.00	
Central House	L.A. & C.M. Driggs	1.75	7.00 to 10.00	
Glen Summit.				
Glen Summit Hotel	Chas. Wenrick	4.00	20.00 to 25.00	325
Wilkes Barre.				
Wyoming Val. Ho.	H. J. Dennin	3.50	15.00 to 21.20	250
Exchange Hotel	A. Whitaker	2.00	10.50	100

Location and Name of Hotel	Proprietor	Rate per Day	Rate per Week	Capacity
Wilkes Barre. (Cont'd.)				
Luzerne Hotel	Geo. W. Ziegler	$2.00	14.00	150
Bristol Hotel	E. C. Wasser	2.00	10.50	100
Courtright Hotel	B. R. Courtright	2.00	9.50	10
Pittston.				
Farnham House	F. F. Farnham	2.00	7.00 to 10.00	40
Eagle Hotel	C. B. Weiser	2.00	8.00 to 10.00	50
Sinclair House	E. M. Sinclair	2.00	7.00 to 10.00	30
Harvey's Lake.				
Lake Hotel	Chas E. Rhoads	2.00	10.00 to 12.00	100
Lake Winola.				
The Winola House	C. E. Frear	2.00	8.00 to 12.00	200
Tunkhannock.				
Wall House	D. C. Graham	2.00	5.00 to 8.00	50
Keeler House	N. Lee	2.00	5.00 to 8.00	50
Warren House	Jas. Donnelly	2.00	5.00 to 8.00	50
Packer House	Billings & Co.	2.00	5.00 to 8.00	50
Stevens House	S. D. Stevens	2.00	5.00 to 8.00	25
Meshoppen.				
Kennard Hotel	Geo. C. Kennard	2.00	7.00 to 12.00	50
Lake Carey.				
Pollner House	H. A. Pollner	2.00	10.00 to 15.00	
Towanda.				
Ward House	Forrest & Chadwick	2.00	5.00 to 8.00	150
Elwell House	O. Kellogg	1.50	4.50	100
Tidd House	E. S. Baker	1.50	7.00	25
Seely House	C. H. Seely	1.50 to 1.50	8.00	125
Sayre.				
Wilbur House	Thos. R. Jordon	2.00	12.00 to 14.00	100
Sayre House	Jas. Beard	2.00	6.00 to 10.00	100
Waverly.				
Tioga Hotel	Hoadley & Powell	2.00	10.00 to 15.00	150
Warford House	S. Wadsworth	2.00	10.00 to 15.00	100
Elmira.				
Rathburn House	H. C. Hayt	3.00	14.00 to 17.00	150
Frazier House	A. J. Dobbins	2.00	14.00	100
Delavan House	J. M. Shomaker & Co.	2.00	14.00	100
Wyckoff House	S. Bowen	2.00	10.50	100
Ithaca.				
Clinton House	S. D. Thompson	2.00	8.00 to 10.00	100
Ithaca Hotel	H. D. Freer	2.00 to 3.00		150
Tompkins House	E. B. Hoagland	1.50	6.00 to 8.00	75
Taghanic Falls.				
Taghanic House	Jno. R. Lytle	2.00 to 2.50	10.00 to 15.00	
Sheldrake.				
Cayuga Lake Ho.	J. J. Lytle	3.00	12.00 to 16.00	250
Cayuga Cottages	J. J. Lytle		10.00	25
Geneva.				
Kirkwood	Goodins & Blaine	2.00	7.00 to 12.00	100
Long Point.				
Long Point Hotel	P. S. Jones	2.00 to 4.00	12.00 to 18.00	200

beauty and exceedingly durable. The feathers of the turkey and goose were more frequently made use of, while the rind of the wild hemp and nettle furnished the twine with which the feathers were ingeniously woven. The *happis*—the band with which they carried their bags and bundles—were also artistically wrought and were exceptionally dumble and strong. After the advent of the white man the skins became a valuable marketable commodity and were disposed of in trade for cloth and woolen goods generally, which in turn became the material from which blankets, shirts and leggings for the males and petticoats for the females were made, a preference given for the colors red, blue and black. Those in good circumstances in life and the young paid great attention to personal appearance, the maidens lining their petticoats with blue or scarlet cloth, while the exterior was fringed with gaily colored ribands or garterings. Their leggings and moccasins were profusely and often artistically embroidered, the decoration being further enhanced by the use of colored porcupine quills. The belles wore little bells or brass thimbles about their ankles, while the beaux wore deers' claws fixed in their knee bands, the object in both sexes being to attract attention and court admiration.

"demi-monde" of that race. For the further enlightment of the young we will refer to the universal want of a beard by the Indians. These, as well as the hairs on the front of the head and up from the neck, were pulled out repeatedly until the hair was literally torn out and the roots destroyed. This was at first accomplished with tweezers made of the muscle shell, later the tweezers were made from spring brass wire, which was always a necessary article of the toilet. The reason assigned for this plucking was that the surface of the skin afforded a better opportunity for tattooing—a means adopted to record the deeds of bravery and heroism. The tattooing was, before the advent of the whites, accomplished by scarifying with sharp flint stones or pricking with the sharp teeth of a fish and laying on a burnt powder obtained from the poplar bark, which was left to dry. Later needles were fixed into a handle, with which the work was done with neatness and dispatch.

massacre at Wyoming 1778

Zeisberger Preaching to the Indians

The women made use of vermilion in painting themselves for dances, but they were circumspect in applying the paint so that it gave no offense or suspicion to husband or lover, for a particular mode of applying the paint was adopted by the

In the old Moravian burying ground at Bethlehem lie the mortal remains of a veteran warrior of the Lenape Nation and Monsey tribe, who was highly regarded by his people and equally dreaded by their enemies. In 1742 he became a convert to the Christian religion and located here with the Christian Indian colony, receiving in baptism the cognomen of *Michael*. Michael was a curiosity and a wonder.

His entire body, or that portion usually exposed and not covered by the scars received in battle, was covered by tattooings depicting the many scenes of carnage and strife in which he had won renown. Face, neck, shoulders, breast, back, arms, thighs and legs bore the record of a truly great warrior, to the amazement of every person who saw him, and while his admirers loved to dwell on his generosity as well as his courage, when asked to relate incidents of his prowess he made answer that "being now taken captive by Jesus Christ it did not become him to relate the deeds he had done while in the service of the Evil Spirit, but that he was willing to give an account of the manner in which he had been conquered."

PHYSICIANS, SURGEONS AND THEIR REMEDIES.

The Indian nations were supposed to have their diseases cured (?) by incantations and jugglery. This was by no means the universal practice, although largely resorted to when the patient was supposed to be afflicted with an evil spirit. The regular practitioners among the more intelligent of the Indian nations were perhaps more free from fanciful theories than those of any other nation on earth. Their science was founded entirely on observation, and they gave much thought and care to the effects of their prescriptions. They were of both sexes, and took great pains to acquire a thorough knowledge of the properties and medicinal virtues of plants, roots and barks for the benefit of their fellow-men. They were also careful to keep a supply constantly on hand, and assiduously gathered and collected, at proper seasons, such as they might need. These were dried and put up in packages and stored for future use.

They were apt to give large doses, believing that much of a good thing must necessarily do much good. Their practice has, however, done much good. Emetics and sweatings were largely resorted to. The wives of missionaries universally accorded great credit to the female practitioners in diseases peculiar to their sex. They were exceedingly apt in healing wounds or bruises. A prescription for a felon was a poultice made from the root of the common blue violet. The result was magical: in less than half an hour the excruciating pain had entirely subsided and the felon vanished. Wounds of a very serious nature were successfully treated. Their *materia medica* was carefully guarded

from strangers. The barks of the white and black oak, the white walnut, the cherry, dogwood, maple, birch and several others, were dried and ground into powder, from which pills were made.

In fevers the Indians usually administered emetics, which were made up and compounded in many ways. Bishop Heckewelder relates seeing a man given an emetic who had poisoned himself with the root of the may-apple. It consisted of a piece of raccoon skin burned with the hair on and finely powdered, to which was added pounded dried beans and gunpowder. These three ingredients were mixed with water and poured down the patient's throat. This brought on a severe vomiting, the poisonous root was entirely discharged and the man saved. In rheumatic affections the patient has recourse to the sweating oven, and, in fact, whenever an Indian felt indisposed he or she at once made use of this mode of treatment. This oven was made of different sizes, usually large enough to accommodate from two to six persons at a time, according to the number of inhabitants in the village. It was generally built on a bank or slope, one half within and the other without the ground. It was well covered on the top with split plank and earth and had a door in front. Here, on the outside, stones, usually the size of a large turnip, were heated by fire by one or more men appointed each day for the purpose. While the oven was being heated decoctions from plants or roots were prepared for the use of the patients. The *pinook* of the public crier brought the patients, each with a small kettle, which was filled for him with a portion of the decoction, serving as a medicine and a creative agent in perspiration. The patients, entering the oven, arranging themselves on either side, the hot stones were placed in the centre and the aperture closed. The tea was now partaken of and the patients remaining therein until the perspiration ceased to flow, when they came out, throwing a blanket about them for protection and going to their tepees, while others similarly afflicted took the vacant places and more hot stones were put in. In severe cases of rheumatism, water was frequently thrown on the hot stones, producing a steam which supposedly increased the heat and gave suppleness to hardened joints and stiff limbs. In some cases the patient was required to take large quantities of a certain decoction and keep wrapped up in his blanket even in the oven. The sweat-ovens were generally some distance from the village, where wood and water were abundant. The best of order was always preserved at those places, the women having separate ovens and in an opposite direction from the village.

"In 1784," says Heckewelder, "a gentleman whom I had known at Detroit, and who had for a long period been in infirm health, came to the village of Christian Indians on the Huron River in

HARVEY'S LAKE.

order to avail himself of the sweat-oven. It being in the middle of the winter, and a deep snow on the ground, the weather was excessively cold. I advised him to postpone his sweating to a warmer season, but he persisted in his resolution. I again advised him by no means to remain in the oven longer than fifteen or at most twenty minutes. But once in and feeling comfortable, he remained a full hour, at the end of which he fainted and was brought by two strong Indians into my house in very great pain, and not able to walk. He remained with me until the next day, when we took him down in his sleigh to his family in Detroit. His situation was truly deplorable. His physicians at that place gave no hopes of his recovery. Suddenly, however, a change took place, and he not only recovered, but became a new man physically, stout, even corpulent, and always insisted that the sweat-oven was the best place for his health he had ever visited. His indisposition had forever left him, from that time until his death, in 1814, at an advanced age."

THE INDIANS AS DARWINIANS.

The Indians looked upon the earth as their universal mother. They said that the good, great and all-powerful Spirit, when He created them, doubtless meant in His own good time to put them in the enjoyment of all the good things which were to be found upon the earth, but He wisely ordained that the first stage of existence should be within it. They are not all agreed as to the form under which they formerly existed. Some believed that they were of human shape, others that they lived in the form of terrestrial animals, such as the groundhog, the rabbit, the tortoise and the rattlesnake, whose names they bore in their tribal relations.

The Delawares maintained that they formerly existed under a lake, and one of their number, discovering an opening from the cavern, crawled out to the surface, where he found a deer, which he took back with him. They killed and ate the deer, pronouncing it food for the gods, and immediately left their subterranean abode for that in the light of day, where such good food was to be had. The other two tribes of this nation, the Unamis, or Tortoise, and the Unalochtigos, or Turkey, had similar ideas of their earlier life, while the Iroquois, a nation entirely unlike the Delawares in habits, dialect and all else, also entertained ideas quite in harmony with the other nations. The tradition prevented the eating of the groundhog or rabbit, for *they were their relations.* The rattlesnake was spared for like reasons, as they considered it their grandfather, who, when danger threatened them, gave the alarm by his rattle. These ancient ideas have been exploded; the Indian of even the last century did not hesitate to kill "the rattler."

The names assumed by tribes of the great nations attest their universal belief in their preëxistence in the form of the animal which in form of heraldry adorned their tepees. Thus the turtle, turkey or wolf appears graphically on houses, blankets, arms, etc., and they are as proud of their origin from the tortoise, the wolf and the turkey as the nobles of Europe are of their descent from the feudal barons of ancient times; and when children sprang from intermarriage between members of different tribes their genealogy was carefully preserved by tradition in the family, that they might know to which tribe they belonged. That they seemed to think that some of their brethren still abided in the form of their earlier existence is manifest in the following, related by the Rev. Zeisberger, a missionary: "A Delaware hunter once shot a huge bear, breaking his backbone, when bruin fell and uttered a plaintive howl. The hunter, instead of giving him another shot, stood close to him and addressed him in the following language: 'Hark, you bear! You are a coward, and no warrior as you pretend to be. Were you a warrior you would show it by your firmness and not cry and whimper like an old woman. You know, bear, that our tribes are at war with each other, and that yours was the aggressor. You have found the Indians too powerful for you, and you have gone sneaking about in the woods, stealing their hogs. Perhaps at this time you have hogflesh in your stomach. Had you conquered me, I would have borne it with courage and died like a brave warrior; but you, bear, sit there and cry and disgrace your tribe by your cowardly conduct.' I

was present at the delivery of this curious invective. When the hunter had dispatched the bear, I asked him if he thought that poor animal could understand what he said? 'Oh!' said he in answer, 'the bear understood me very well. Did you not observe how ashamed he looked while I upbraided him?'"

INDIAN COMPUTATION OF TIME.

The Indians did not reckon as we do, by days and nights. They said, "It is —— nights traveling to —— place." "I shall return home in —— night," etc. Pointing to the heavens, they would say, "You will see me again when the sun stands there." Their year was, like ours, divided into four parts: spring, summer, autumn and winter. It began with the spring, which they called the youth of the year, the season when the spirits of the man begin to revive and the plants and flowers again put forth. These seasons were again sub-divided into months, or *moons,* each of which had a particular name, yet not the same among all the tribes and nations, these denominations being generally adapted to the climate under which they respectively lived and the advantages and benefits they enjoyed at the time. Thus the Lenape, while they inhabited the country bordering on the Atlantic, called March the "*shad* moon," because these fish at that time begin to pass from the sea into the rivers, where they deposit their spawn; but, as there is no such fish in the country into which they afterwards removed, they changed the name of that month to "running of the *sap* moon." April was the "*spring* moon;" May the "*planting* moon;" June the "*fawn* moon," from the fact that the deer bring forth their young in this month, and again, the deer change their color to a reddish hue. July was called the "*summer* moon;" August "*roasting ears* moon," from the fact that the corn is fit to roast; September the "*autumn* moon;" October the "*harvest* moon;" December the "*hunting* moon," it being the season when stags have dropped their antlers or horns. January was called the "*mouse* or *squirrel* moon," because at this season these animals leave their holes. February the "*frog* moon," because, on warm days, the frogs begin to croak. Some nations called the month of January by a name which denoted the "sun returns," probably because the days begin to lengthen at that time. When the leaf of the white oak had budded and become the size of the ear of a mouse the corn planting season had arrived. The arrival of the whip-poor-will and its call at the same season led to the idiom *hackiheck!*

They calculated their ages by some remarkable event which had taken place within their remembrance, as, for instance, an uncommonly severe winter, a very deep snow, an extraordinary freshet, a general war, the building of a new city or town by the white people.

PERTINENT THOUGHTS ON OUR WATER.

OUR WATER SUPPLY.

There has been for some years a growing demand for a more adequate supply of *pure* water. This demand does not come from any one or two particular sections; but as our population increases the necessity becomes more urgent in all sections, and those for the welfare of which THE COMET labors need fully as much thought and care as any others. We assert, in an off-handed way, that man can not live without water. Scientists, especially those devoted to hygiene, tell us that water must be pure, or it becomes a source of death instead of life.

When it is more generally known that water is an all-important agency for the digestion and assimilation of food, that 75 per cent. of the human body is composed of water, that four and one-half pounds are thrown off daily by a healthy body, and that a diet largely nitrogenous will tax the system severely unless a considerable quantity of water be taken for the purpose of getting rid of the waste, some more serious attention will be given to the water supply for our municipalities. It is estimated that a full-grown male adult requires fifty-two fluid ounces of water daily. It is then self-evident that an adequate supply of pure water should be a theme of vital importance, primarily, in the minds of our people, and more particularly in the minds of our representative bodies.

ORIGIN OF SUPPLY.

In the beginning of time the edict to "Let the waters be gathered together into one place and let the dry land appear," established the law of supply and demand. From Old Ocean, salt though he be and foul, nature drinks in great quantities, and in its own good way purifies it, eliminating the undesirable elements, when it is given to us in the rainfall, soft and pure beyond a question of doubt. The earth and its component parts now enter into

the question of purity. The impermeable strata shed the water and it flows into declivities, forming lakes. The permeable strata receive the flow of water, and by absorption carry it into the earth, until it strikes another impermeable stratum, when the water is forced along this stratum until at some point it bubbles forth a "sparkling spring." Just to the extent that the water, associated with minerals on its way through the earth, is it a mineral spring. The lakes and springs, in turn, are the cause of and supply the streams and rivers.

SOURCES OF SUPPLY.

The simplest method of procuring pure water is to collect the rain as it falls from the clouds. In the limestone region of the Lehigh Valley, known for a century and a half as the "Dryland," this has been the popular method adopted for a water supply, and since the advent of slate is still more highly regarded. The modern cistern is indeed a blessing; it is a cemented stone vault in one corner of the cellar. The cistern floor is possibly ten feet below that of the cellar, and the walls of the cistern extend upward possibly four feet above the floor of the cellar, the covering of the cistern being slate slabs perfectly joined. Accessory to this, which may be termed the storage vault, is another but very much smaller cistern or receiving vault, the floor of which is no deeper than the top of the main cistern or storage vault. The smaller or receiving vault is supplied with a deposit of charcoal, through which all the water collected from the roof of the building passes before it is deposited in the larger or storage vault. The good housekeeper carefully guards the roof of her home and keeps the water "turned off" until the roof is thoroughly clean from dust, etc., when she will turn the water-switch and allow it to run into the cistern. A cistern should be sufficiently large to permit of storing enough water during the winter months to tide over the heated term. The slate slab top, being about four feet above the floor of the cellar, is readily adaptable as a refrigerator.

SPRINGS.

A very valuable source of water supply is provided by springs. These springs appear at the lowest point of the outcrop of a permeable stratum where it rests upon an impermeable stratum, and they constitute the outflow of the rain which has percolated through that stratum. A spring is generally clear and free from organic impurities, as particles in suspension are removed by the natural filtration, and organic matters are oxidized and eliminated in the passage of the water through the ground. When, as frequently happens, the water is strongly impregnated with certain substances as to receive specific names, these springs are of more value for medicinal purposes than as a water supply.

WELLS.

There are two kinds of wells, namely, the shallow well, sunk into a superficial permeable stratum, and the deep or artesian well, the name applied to water springs rising above the surface of the ground by natural hydrostatic pressure on boring a small hole down through a series of strata to a water-carrying bed enclosed between two impervious layers. Shallow wells, while they may be ample and desirable to supply a scattered populace, are exceedingly undesirable in a community, because of the exposure to the worst forms of contamination.

STREAMS AND RIVERS.

The streams of the Lehigh, Schuylkill, Wyoming and Susquehanna Valleys are in like condition with the streams and rivers of all other densely populated portions of our too free America, not as pure and free from contamination as we would wish them or as they should be, for thousands upon thousands depend upon them for a water supply.

SOURCES OF CONTAMINATION.

The springs and wells of our valleys, like the springs and wells of all other sections, are subject to pollution from surface drainage and filterings from improperly constructed cesspools. The springs in the mountains, notably those at our summer resorts, furnish a delicious, pure and invigorating water. The frequency of wells in the more densely populated mining and industrial districts inspires a feeling of uncertainty and a dread of natural consequences incident upon the rudely built cesspools and an utter disregard for proper sanitary measures. Nor are we to believe that the large manufacturing towns, even with the most approved sanitary plumbing and a modern sewerage, are exempt from the evils attendant upon an inadequate water supply and an imperfect drainage.

We are, comparatively speaking, supremely blest with facilities for a bountiful supply of *pure* water, and if man will attend to the making of the town, as God made the country, all will be well.

SEWERAGE.

A good and pure water supply in a densely populated district implies a thorough and just system of sewerage as well. The two are inseparably connected. The present system of sewerage is justly condemned by the State Board of Health. No individual or municipality has a moral or legal right to pollute the streams by pouring or dumping into them his or its offal and excrement, thereby causing the waters to be unfit for use by the inhabitants on the stream farther down. Under the caption of "sewerage" there appeared an editorial in the

BASS FISHING ON THE UPPER SUSQUEHANNA.

Country Doctor which was thought worthy of reproduction by the *Annals of Hygiene*, and we, deeming it worthy of the greatest publicity, insert it here:

"The great sanitary problem of the future is the disposal of the sewage of our large cities in some other and better manner than furnishing it to our neighbors below to drink. It does seem that some inventive genius could hit upon a plan that would be equal to the task of returning this vast amount of waste to the soil where it belongs, in the shape of a cheap fertilizer, and thus keep up the productiveness of the soil and protect the health at one and the same time. Millions upon millions of dollars' worth of the best fertilizing agent known is annually thrown into our streams to pollute their waters with disease producing germs that ought to be utilized in restoring impoverished lands in the vicinity and increasing and cheapening the food supply of the people. There is a large fortune in store for the one who devises a practical plan for utilizing sewage as a fertilizer; and more, he will be the greatest humanitarian and philanthropist of the age."

We do not realize how a patent could be obtained on a system or method that every person must adopt for himself individually to secure the boon so earnestly desired by the *Country Doctor* and others of like minds, but we do know that if the only authorized cesspool and water-closet vault was constructed upon the plan of a cistern, walled and cemented and quicklime used at frequent periods as a disinfectant and deodorizer, being emptied twice annually by the odorless method now universal, the refuse taken to and put in vats to which the siftings of coal ashes (the disposal of which is often a matter for serious consideration) be added, the hoped for result by the *Country Doctor* and others would be accomplished and the costly, death-dealing sewerage system of the present would be abolished, while our lakes, rivers and streams would furnish an adequate supply of good, pure and wholesome water for all.

SPARKS ALONG THE LINE.

—GLEN ONOKO has received much attention since the close of last season. The many admirers of this truly wonderful resort will be pleased because of the increased accommodation.

—"SEASICKNESS" on the railroad is an affliction that many are subjected to: for such traveling is no pleasure. If the susceptible will provide themselves with strong peppermint lozenges, and make use of them at such times, immediate relief is assured.

—POTTSVILLE is after more water and is determined to have it, notwithstanding the emphatic "No" of the many would-be owners of the Tumbling Run water shed. Good, pure water is a necessity, and Pottsville should have it.

—ALLENTOWN is just now exercised about the insufficiency of its water supply and is about making provision for an extension, and there seem to be serious objections to proposed methods. Go slow, gentlemen. First find you are right, then go ahead.

—IT IS A SINGULAR FACT that the first Bible published in America was in the Indian language—Mohegan (Mohican) dialect. It was translated into the Indian by John Elliott and published by Samuel Green and Marmaduke Johnson, at Cambridge, Mass., in 1663.

—THE PRESIDENT, the mammoth engine at the Friedensville zinc mines, just over the mountains from South Bethlehem,

Pa., is again at work and will be one of the important attractions for summer guests who seek rest and recreation in the beautiful town of Bethlehem.

—GLEN SUMMIT.—That Glen Summit is an exceedingly popular mountain resort is manifest by the constant additions required. The hotel has again been enlarged and an electric plant added. The walks and drives have all received attention, and the house is fast filling up with full-season guests.

—KIMBALL'S ISLAND at Laury's has been taken in charge by the Lehigh Valley Railroad Company. A number of Sunday Schools have already been booked for excursions.—*Ex.* This island is one of the prettiest on the line of the Lehigh Valley Railroad and is fully equipped to thoroughly meet the wants of picnic excursions, with pavilions, kitchen, swings etc.

—THE city of Scranton is somewhat exercised because of certain methods attending the conduct of the People's Street Railway. Scranton is looked upon as being the city of first importance *electrically*, and from what we know of Col. Price, the champion of the people's rights, we have reason to believe that the People's Street Railway will be run in the interests of the PEOPLE as well as for the People's *Street Railway.*

[Copy.]

DARTMOUTH COLLEGE, HANOVER, N. H., June 11, 1891.

Dear Sir: I beg to thank you for the copies of THE COMET, an interesting and valuable publication, giving proof of no small care and labor in preparation. Its contents (or their contents) is just what I want. I hope to verify soon in person. Yours very truly, R. FLETCHER, Professor, Thayer School of Engineering.

E. B. BYINGTON, G.P.A., Lehigh Valley Railroad.

—THE WINOLA, situated on the beautiful lake of the same name in Wyoming County, Pa., promises additional conveniences and comforts this season. This hotel has always been a popular resort, growing more so season after season until it was compelled to spread itself. This it did last season, and was, in consequence, even more popular. Mr. C. E. Frear, the genial proprietor, is determined to merit the continuance of favors shown his house, and has increased the facilities of the Winola, thereby giving his guests additional comforts and conveniences.

—TO SAVE BOSTON HALF A MILLION A YEAR.—Mr. Ernest W. Bowditch, the well-known engineer, who for the past year has been investigating the methods employed in carrying on the various city departments, as authorized by the Citizens' Association, has published his report. The result of his inquiry shows a general plan for the reorganization of the departments and the placing of them under one management, by which it is believed a saving of $450,000 a year can be effected.—*Ex.*

This is a "pointer" to the municipalities of the Lehigh, Schuylkill, Wyoming and Susquehanna Valleys.

—THE new and commodious pavilion at Harvey's Lake is being rapidly pushed to completion by Contractor Shepherd and his large force of men. Our predictions last season are now admitted by all who go there, and we feel justified in reiterating them. Harvey's Lake is fast becoming *the* mountain lake resort of Pennsylvania. Three steamers now ply its waters. Excursions and picnics are well provided for. The The scenery, ferns, rocks, lichen and forest are simply GRAND. The site for the large and commodious hotel in prospective has finally been decided upon and work may begin at any time.

—THE Editorial Association of Schuylkill County, composed of editors and editresses, recently excursed to Harvey's Lake and after their return were impelled to a half column's expatiation upon the beauties of the route, the excellence of the service given by the Lehigh Valley Railroad and the picturesqueness of the scenery about the lake. Were they so disposed they could devote a page to Harvey's Lake and environment and yet not half would be told. The remarkable fern and lichen, shady walks and drives must be seen to be appreciated.

—WELL, WHAT OF IT?—"Wedded a Sioux," "Romance of a Poetess,"are two of the flaming headlines that greet the eye of the reader, in the daily and weekly papers in this month of mating and roses.

If there had been a few Miss Goodales in the beginning of the eighteenth century, when the Indian was a laborer in the iron mills on the Schuylkill; if the white man had dealt with the red man half fairly, endeavoring to make a place for him in our midst and helping him to accommodate himself to the new order of things, we would today have no "Indian question" confronting us; no agencies (?) to rob both the Indian and the National Treasury, but one people from the Atlantic to the Pacific, better, nobler and more thoroughly American.

—COMMENCEMENT.—The papers are full of it. The air resounds with it. Essays and gifts, diplomas and flowers, ending with banquets and song. The important college graduate with his "sheepskin," the sweet girl graduate with her "doeskin," glad to escape the fetters that bind, rush headlong into the meshes of hard every-day life. Commencement to them has come and gone, the school days are over and another commencement is being made. Will the end be as victorious? Life means more than the young usually care to believe, and it has many pitfalls to be shunned as well as successes to be attained. The race is not always given to the swift. The brightest graduate of his class at the end of a decade is sometimes, yes often, found at the bottom, while the prosaic and plodding carves his way to the zenith.

Mr. Oldrad (class of '60)—"Ah, this is our class picture. Ah, old boy, we were younger then than we are now." Mr. De Gree—"Yes, and knew a great deal more."—Brooklyn Life.

—PAXINOSA INN, Easton, Pa., has added to its importance and scenic beauty again for this season. The lovely walks and drives have been extended to many more spots in its environment, all of which teem with the romance of Indian legend and colonial history. The memorable spot where in 1757 the Great Council was held, in which three hundred representative warriors took part; where the renowned Teedyuscung, chief of the Lenapes, and Paxinosa, king of the Shawnees, delivered addresses that startled their hearers, is to be seen from the piazza.

The inn with its new addition is now 350 feet in length and offers unequaled accommodation to its guests. Mr. Charles A. Stone, than whom there is none better, is again at the helm and we feel warranted in saying the season of "'01" will eclipse both former seasons, in which the hostelry gained an enviable reputation.

—LAKE CAREY.—This popular resort is already well filled with summer guests. Lake Carey is, next to Harvey's Lake, the largest body of water in Pennsylvania and is located four miles from Tunkhannock, on the line of the Lehigh Valley Railroad. The many beautiful cottages which nestle among the rich verdure by which the lake is surrounded are being gradually occupied, almost every day bringing one or more who make this charming resort their home during the heated term. The hotel, owned by Dr. E. L. Diefenderfer, of Ashley, is being enlarged and generally improved. An addition for dancing purposes and other amusements has been built, and the landlord, L. E. Meade, will soon be nicely situated to accommodate either the large number of transient guests who will seek entertainment there or the many permanents who are sure to be with him for the season. He sets an elegant table, the house is well appointed throughout, cool and comfortable in the hottest weather, while its situation is such as to command a fine view of the lake, so that those who do not wish to participate in the pleasures that always await on the water may loll in the shade of the spacious veranda and witness the enjoyment of the others. The spring at the hotel is a valuable adjunct of the place. The water is clear as crystal, pure as purity itself, is the next thing to ice water in coolness and a delight to all.

There are plenty of boats, both at the private cottages and at the hotel, and it is a great place for rowing and fishing, and, on warm moonlight nights, for music on the waters. But there will be more of this later on, when the cottages are all occupied and the season is at its height, which will be in the months of July and August.

EXCURSIONS OVER THE LEHIGH VALLEY.

—SOCIETIES OF THE ARMY OF THE POTOMAC, at Buffalo, July 3 and 4. 1⅓ fares, on certificates.

—NORTHEASTERN SÆNGERBUND, at Newark, N. J. One fare for the round trip. Tickets good going from July 2 to 4; returning from July 2 to 10, inclusive.

—BAPTIST YOUNG PEOPLE'S NATIONAL CONVENTION, at Chicago. 1⅓ fares on certificates, July 7 and 8.

—YOUNG PEOPLE'S SOCIETY OF CHRISTIAN ENDEAVOR, Minneapolis, Minn. Single fare for round trip. Tickets good going from July 6 to 8; returning, July 12 to 15, inclusive. Via the Popular Lehigh Valley Railroad, leaving New York at 8.10 A.M., and Philadelphia at 9 A.M.

—NATIONAL EDUCATIONAL ASSOCIATION, at Toronto, Ont. July 14 to 17. Single fare for the round trip.

—SEMI-ANNUAL ENCAMPMENT, G. A. R., Department of Pennsylvania, at Williamsport, Pa. July 11 to 18. Single fare for the round trip, on cards.

—PHOTOGRAPHERS' ASSOCIATION OF AMERICA, at Buffalo. July 14 to 17. 1⅓ fares on certificate.

—AMATEUR (NATIONAL) PRESS ASSOCIATION, at Philadelphia. July 14 to 18. 1⅓ fares on certificate.

—PATRIOTIC ORDER OF TRUE AMERICANS, at Reading, Pa. July 21 to 23, on card orders.

—ANNUAL ENCAMPMENT, G.A.R, at Detroit, Mich. August 3 to 8.

—C. T. A. UNION OF AMERICA, at Washington, D. C. August 5 to 7. 1⅓ fares on certificate.

—NATIONAL BAR ASSOCIATION OF THE UNITED STATES, at Nantucket Beach, Mass. 1⅓ fares on certificates.

—GRAND LODGE, KNIGHTS OF PYTHIAS OF PENNA., at Harrisburg. August 18, on card orders.

—HAZLETON is determined to eclipse all attempts heretofore made in Central Pennsylvania in celebrating the "Glorious Fourth." Scranton will send 400. Wilkes Barre and surrounding towns will swell the throng to a thousand or more, while Pottsville, Shenandoah, Mauch Chunk, and other towns down the valley will join with the suburban towns in swelling the mass of celebrants several more thousands.

L.V.

⟶❋ LEHIGH ✛ VALLEY ✛ RAILROAD ❋⟵

DOUBLE TRACK.

✛AMERICA'S✛WONDERLAND.✛

The Popular Route between New York, Philadelphia, Baltimore, Washington
and Easton, Bethlehem, Allentown, Mauch Chunk, Pottsville, Wilkes
Barre, Pittston, Scranton, Ithaca, Geneva, Waverly, Watkins
Glen, Elmira, Rochester, Buffalo, Niagara Falls,
Toronto, Detroit,

CHICAGO, ST. LOUIS AND ALL POINTS WEST.

Pullman Palace Buffet Cars and Chair Cars on all Through Trains.

NO SMOKE } *THE MOUNTAIN AND VALLEY SCENERY TRAVERSED by this line is the most beautiful and picturesque in America, embracing the* { **NO DUST**
Romantic Valleys of the Susquehanna and Lehigh, and the Historic Wyoming. ANTHRACITE COAL IS USED EXCLU-
SIVELY, thus avoiding the dense volumes of smoke that so terribly annoy passengers on lines using Bituminous Coal.

TICKET OFFICES:

NEW YORK:—GENERAL EASTERN OFFICE, 235 BROADWAY; Depot, foot of Courtlandt Street; Depot, foot of Desbrosses Street, and all principal Pennsylvania
Railroad Ticket Offices.

PHILADELPHIA:—836 Chestnut Street; Philadelphia & Reading Depots, Ninth and Green and
Third and Berks Streets.

BUFFALO:—Corner of Main and Seneca Streets.

THROUGH CAR SERVICE ARRANGEMENT.

WESTWARD.

TRAIN No. 31.—Day Coach Phillipsburg to Harrisburg.
TRAIN No. 19.—Day Coach Phillipsburg to Reading, and Phila-
delphia to Avoca.
TRAIN No. 21.—Day Coaches New York to Mauch Chunk.
TRAIN No. 2.—Pullman Parlor Car Philadelphia to Buffalo
and Suspension Bridge. Chair Car New York
to Lyons. Day Coaches Philadelphia and New
York to Buffalo, and Philadelphia to Scranton.
TRAIN No. 4.—Day Coaches New York to Mauch Chunk, and
Phillipsburg to Harrisburg.
TRAIN No. 16.—Day Coach New York to Elmira and Easton to
Hazleton.
TRAIN No. 20.—Day Coach Phillipsburg to Reading.
TRAIN No. 6.—Chair Car and Day Coach New York to Tunk-
hannock. Chair Car Philadelphia to Wilkes
Barre. Day Coach Philadelphia to Tunkhan-
nock.
TRAIN No. 12.—Chair Car New York to Wilkes Barre and Day
Coach New York to L. & B. Junct. Chair Car
Philadelphia to Hazleton. Day Coaches Phila-
delphia to Wilkes Barre and Scranton.
TRAIN No. 44.—Chair Car and Day Coaches New York to
Pottsville.
TRAIN No. 28.—Day Coaches New York to Mauch Chunk, and
Phillipsburg to Harrisburg.
TRAIN No. 8.—Pullman Buffet Sleeping Cars New York and
Philadelphia to Lyons, Buffalo and Suspension
Bridge. Day Coaches New York and Philadel-
phia to Buffalo.

SUNDAY TRAIN No. 2.—Day Coaches New York to Hazleton
and Philadelphia to Mauch Chunk.
SUNDAY TRAIN No. 16.—Through Day Coaches New York to
Hazleton.

EASTWARD.

TRAIN No. 15.—Pullman Buffet Sleeping Cars, Suspension
Bridge, Buffalo and Lyons to Philadelphia and
New York. Day Coaches Buffalo to Philadel-
phia and New York.
TRAIN No. 17.—Day Coaches Mauch Chunk to New York.
TRAIN No. 45.—Chair Car and Day Coaches Pottsville to New
York.
TRAIN No. 21.—Chair Car and Day Coaches L. & B. Junct. to
New York. Chair Car Hazleton to Philadelphia.
Day Coach L. & B. Junct. to Philadelphia.
TRAIN No. 1.—Day Coach Harrisburg to Redington.
TRAIN No. 23.—Day Coaches L. & B. Junction and Hazleton to
New York.
TRAIN No. 3.—Chair Car and Day Coach Tunkhannock to New
York. Day Coaches Scranton and Tunkhan-
nock to Philadelphia.
TRAIN No. 30.—Day Coach Reading to Phillipsburg.
TRAIN No. 25.—Day Coach Harrisburg to Phillipsburg.
TRAIN No. 5.—Chair Cars Lyons to New York and Wilkes Barre
to Philadelphia. Day Coaches Elmira to New
York and Scranton to Philadelphia.
TRAIN No. 27.—Day Coach Harrisburg to Phillipsburg.
TRAIN No. 7.—Day Coaches Wilkes Barre to New York and
Philadelphia.
TRAIN No. 13.—Day Coach Reading to Phillipsburg.
TRAIN No. 9.—Pullman Parlor Car Suspension Bridge and
Buffalo to Philadelphia. Day Coaches Buffalo
to Philadelphia and New York.

SUNDAY No. 23.—Through Day Coaches Hazleton to New York.
SUNDAY No. 7.—Day Coach Hazleton and Avoca to New York,
and Mauch Chunk to Philadelphia.

FAST NIGHT EXPRESS.

LEHIGH VALLEY SOLID TRAIN (Eastlake and
Pullman Buffet Sleeping Cars) through between NEW
YORK or PHILADELPHIA and LYONS or BUFFALO
and SUSPENSION BRIDGE (DAILY), connecting with
the Michigan Central, Lake Shore, New York, Chicago &
St. Louis and Grand Trunk Railways for TORONTO and
all points in Canada; DETROIT, CLEVELAND, CIN-
CINNATI, CHICAGO, ST. LOUIS, and all points West.
Leave New York 7.30 P. M., Philadelphia 8.30 P. M., arriving at Buffalo 8.45 A.M., Suspension Bridge 11.00 A. M.
Returning, leave Suspension Bridge 4.45 P. M., Buffalo
5.30 P. M., arriving at Philadelphia 7.04 A. M., New York
8.00 A.M.

FAST DAY EXPRESS.

LEHIGH VALLEY SOLID TRAIN, thoroughly
equipped with the most modern Pullman Buffet Parlor
Cars, expressly made for this Company, through between
NEW YORK or PHILADELPHIA and LYONS or BUF-
FALO and SUSPENSION BRIDGE (daily except Sun-
days), connecting with the Michigan Central, Lake Shore
and Grand Trunk Railways for TORONTO and all points
in Canada; DETROIT, CLEVELAND, CINCINNATI,
CHICAGO, ST. LOUIS, and all points West. Leaves New
York 8.10 A. M., Philadelphia 9.00 A.M., arriving at Buffalo 10.35 P. M., Suspension Bridge 12.10 night. Returning, leave Suspension Bridge 8.30 A.M., Buffalo 9.10 A.M.,
arriving at Philadelphia 9.55 P.M., New York 10.50 P.M.

LEHIGH VALLEY RAILROAD.

GENERAL OFFICERS AND HEADS OF DEPARTMENTS, JANUARY 1st, 1891.

E. P. WILBUR,
President.

H. S. DRINKER,
Gen. Counsel and Asst. to Prest.

WM. STEVENSON,
Gen. Northern Supt.

WM. H. SAYRE,
Genl. Coal Agent.

CHAS. E. WEBSTER,
Asst. Chief Engineer.

JAMES DONNELLY,
Supt. New Jersey Div.

JOHN H. HECKMAN,
Genl. Freight Agent.

P. C. DOYLE,
G. N. Frt. and Pass. Agent.

ASA P. BLAKSLEE,
Genl. Car Agent.

C. H. WEBB,
Auditor Through Freights.

JOHN NICHOL,
Lost and Damaged Freight Agt.

JOHN I. KINSEY,
Master Mechanic.

J. N. WEAVER,
Master Mechanic.

W. J. POWERS,
Supt. Morris Canal.

CHAS. HARTSHORNE,
Vice President.

ROLLIN H. WILBUR,
Asst. to and Vice President.

W. C. ALDERSON,
Treasurer.

E. B. BYINGTON,
Genl. Passenger Agent.

J. I. BLAKSLEE,
Supt. Coal Branches.

A. P. BLAKSLEE,
Supt. Pottsville Div.

W. S. SPEIRS,
Asst. Genl. Freight Agent.

A. W. NONNEMACHER,
Genl. Ticket Agent.

E. Y. HARTSHORNE,
Asst. Purchasing Agent.

JOHN GREEN,
Auditor Local Freights.

S. G. COLLINS,
Road Auditor.

DAVID CLARK,
Master Mechanic.

JOHN S. LENTZ,
Supt. Car Dept.

F. H. JANVIER,
Ass't General Counsel.

ROBERT H. SAYRE,
2nd Vice President.

JOHN TAYLOR,
Genl. Traffic Manager.

JOHN R. FANSHAWE,
Secretary.

ISAAC McQUILKIN,
Comptroller.

A. PARDEE,
Supt. Hazleton Div.

H. D. TITUS,
Supt. So. Central Div.

T. J. KLASE,
Genl. Eastern Freight Agent.

W. B. SMITH,
Genl. Eastern Pass. Agent.

J. H. WILHELM,
Paymaster.

W. W. WEAVER,
Actg. Auditor Coal Freights.

CAPT. W. P. HENRY,
Genl. Mgr. L. V. Trans. Co.

CHARLES DEWITT,
Master Mechanic.

W. F. PASCOE,
Supt. of Bridges.

J. F. SCHAPERKOTTER,
Real Estate Agent.

JOHN B. GARRETT,
3d Vice President.

H. STANLEY GOODWIN,
Genl. Eastern Supt.

ISRAEL W. MORRIS,
Assistant Secretary.

A. W. STEDMAN,
Chief Engineer.

A. MITCHELL,
Supt. Wyoming Div.

W. A. LATHROP,
Supt. of Mines.

BERT. HAYDEN,
Division Freight Agent.

N. VAN HORN,
Genl. S. E. Pass. Agent.

GEO. H. HAINES,
Asst. Paymaster.

CHAS. E. AMIDON,
Freight Claim Agent.

F. B. MORRIS,
G. Mr. P. A. Towing Line.

JOHN CAMPBELL,
Master Mechanic.

J. H. JACOBY,
Acting Supt. of Telegraph.

R. M. BRODHEAD,
Division Pass. Agent

C. A. BLOOD,
Division Freight Agent.

LEHIGH VALLEY TRANSPORTATION CO.

CAPT. W. P. HENRY, GENERAL MANAGER, BUFFALO, N. Y.

STEWART MURRAY, General Western Agent, Chicago, Ill.
W. N. HAUGH, Contracting Agt., Chicago, Ill.
C. A. WILLIAMS, Contracting Agent, Milwaukee, Wis.

P. R. JARVIS, Agt., Corn Exchange Bldg., Minneapolis, Minn.
G. H. ABBOTT, Cont'g Agt., 111 Bond Street, New York.
T. J. WILBEE, Agent, Buffalo, N. Y.

SOLICITING AGENTS.

GEO. W. MITCHELL, Agt., 836 Chestnut St., Philadelphia, Pa.
THOS. L. PAINTER, South Bethlehem, Pa.
P. J. FERGUSON, Shenandoah, Pa.
CHAS. A. SMITH, Hazleton, Pa.
JOHN W. LYONS, Rochester, N. Y.
E. W. DRINKER, 809 Lackawanna Ave., Scranton, Pa.
JOHN S. HARTZELL, Allentown, Pa.

JOHN S. HUNT, Flemington, N. J.
F. W. LYON, Auburn, N. Y.
H. B. SMITH, Elmira, N. Y.
D. D'c. COOPER, Canadian Agent, Toronto, Ont.
GEO. L. DOUGHTY, Passenger Agent, 235 Broadway, N.Y.
H. B. MOORE, Foreign Frt. Agt., Room 6, Produce Exchange.
G. W. SHELDON & CO., Import Frt. Agt., 81 New St., N.Y. [N.Y.

THROUGH FREIGHT LINE AGENCIES.—TRADERS' DESPATCH LINE.

T. N. JARVIS, MANAGER, BUFFALO, N. Y.

F. C. HOVEY, Agent, 235 Broadway, New York.
J. H. GILBERT, Contracting Agent, 235 Broadway, New York.
J. C. ELDREDGE, Con'g Agent, 235 Broadway, New York.
I. J. BASSETT, Agent, 250 Washington Street, Boston, Mass.
E. E. JOHNSON, Agent, Worcester, Mass.
GEO. W. MITCHELL, Agent, 836 Chestnut St., Philadelphia, Pa.
P. M. DIVER, Cont'g Agt., 836 Chestnut St., Philadelphia, Pa.
W. E. KEATING, Agent, 501 Broadway, Albany, N. Y.
THOS. J. WILBEE, Cont'g Agent, 228 Main Street, Buffalo, N.Y.
JOHN A. ROSE, Cont'g Agent, 28 Exchange Street, Buffalo, N.Y.
H. ALLEN, Traveling Agent, Cleveland, Ohio.
F. H. BAKER, Agent, 221 Bank Street, Cleveland, Ohio.
R. H. CAMPBELL, Agent, 131 E. Third Street, Dayton, Ohio.
F. W. BENT, Agent, Chamber of Com. Bldg., Cincinnati, Ohio.
J. V. STANBERRY, Agent, 28 Chamber of Commerce Bldg., Indianapolis, Ind.

L. BRIGGS, Agt., Room 214, First Nat. Bank Bldg., Omaha, Neb.
C. R. RUSSEL, Agent, Memphis, Tenn.
A. J. BARNIDGE, Agent, 315 Olive Street, St. Louis, Mo.
F. W. STOCKTON, West Bound Agt., 315 Olive St., St. Louis, Mo.
T. L. LaFLANEILIS, Agent, 187 La Salle Street, Chicago, Ill.
HOWARD WHIPPLE, Cont'g Agt., 187 La Salle Street, Chicago, Ill.
E. A. EDGAR, Traveling Agent, 187 La Salle Street, Chicago, Ill.
CHAS. D. PARKER, Agent, St. Paul and Minneapolis, Minn.
F. G. SMITH, Agent, 201 "The Exchange," Kansas City, Mo.
F. MULDEN, 14 Chamber of Commerce, Peoria, Ill.
R. H. RUDD, Agent, 127 St. Ann Street, Owensboro, Ky.
J. L. ROOT, Agent, Keokuk, Iowa.
V. Z. ROBINSON, Agent, Burlington, Iowa.
N. C. TREAT, Agent, Quincy, Ill.

LEHIGH & WABASH DESPATCH LINE.

M. L. DOHERTY, MANAGER, DETROIT, MICH.

W. H. BURGESS, Agent, 235 Broadway, New York.
THOS. C. DOAN, Cont'g Agent, 235 Broadway, New York.
GEO. W. MITCHELL, Agent, 836 Chestnut St., Philadelphia, Pa.
JAMES E. SULGER, Cont'g Agent, 836 Chestnut Street,
Philadelphia, Pa.
C. L. LYON, Traveling Agent, 836 Chestnut St., Philadelphia, Pa.
H. DEAN, Agent, Room 222, Hammond Building, Detroit, Mich.
W. O. McCRAE, Cont'g Agent, Detroit, Mich.
H. A. LOUDON, Agent, 109 Royal Insurance Building,
Chicago, Ill.

C. F. WATKINS, Cont'g Agent, 109 Royal Insurance Building,
Chicago, Ill.
A. LOVINGSTON, Agent, Continental Building, St. Louis, Mo.
L. W. FROST, Agent, No. 70 Kilby Street, Boston, Mass.
P. J. TAPP, Agent, Board of Trade Bldg., Kansas City, Mo.
ALFRED WHITE, Nor. Western Agent,
82 Chamber of Commerce, Milwaukee, Wis.
T. M. CHIVINGTON, Agent,
Chamber of Commerce, Minneapolis, Minn.

THE ONLY LINE by which passengers can leave SUSPENSION BRIDGE
and BUFFALO on Sunday afternoon, and reach Philadelphia,
Baltimore and Washington on Monday morning.

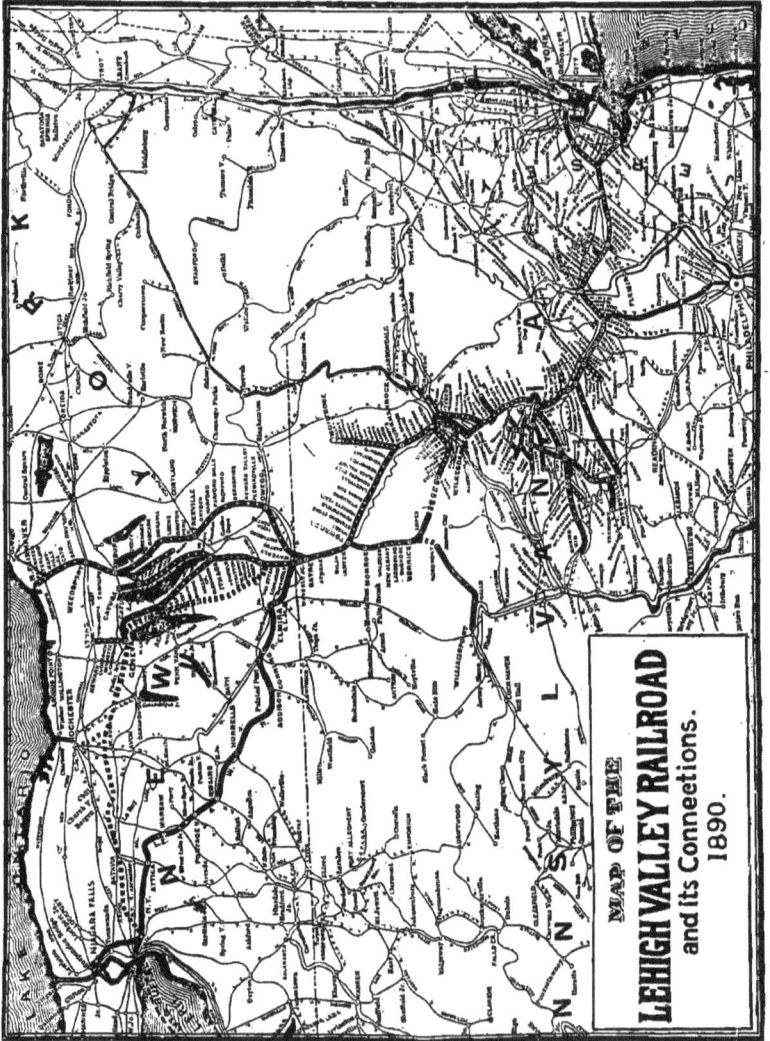

MAP OF THE
LEHIGH VALLEY RAILROAD
and its Connections.
1890.

ALL TRAINS OF THE LEHIGH VALLEY are run directly into the heart of
the City of Philadelphia (Ninth and Green Streets Depot). New York Terminus,
Pennsylvania R. R. Depot, foot of Courtlandt or Desbrosses Street.

www.ingramcontent.com/pod-product-compliance
Lightning Source LLC
Chambersburg PA
CBHW021608270326
41931CB00009B/1389